AND THE BEAT GOES ON

...AT
MY...
...PACE

And the Beat Goes On
At my Pace

Copyright © 2019 by Joe Allen, Jr.

Urban Centigrade®
751 East 161st Street
Bronx, NY 10456
www.urbancentigrade.com
Email: wamuhu.mwaura@urbancentigrade.com

Urban Centigrade® logo is proprietary and copyright protected. Designed by Antony Kamau.

Front and back cover image: Peter Griffin, CC0 (PUBLIC DOMAIN). Lettering and interior design by Wamuhu Mwaura. Author photograph provided by Joe Allen, Jr.

Ordering Information, quantity sales:

Special discounts are available on quantity purchases by individuals, small businesses, and localized retailers. For details, contact the publisher at the address above. Orders by U.S. trade bookstores and wholesalers, please contact publisher via e-mail above.

ISBN: 978-0-9903043-5-7

Printed in the United States of America

AND THE BEAT GOES ON

AT MY PACE

POETIC WORKS BY

JOE ALLEN, JR.

EDITED BY WAMUHU MWAURA

URBAN CENTIGRADE®
NEW YORK

Also Available from Urban Centigrade

by Joe Allen, Jr.
PROGRESSION
STILL BREATHING

‡

by Wamuhu Mwaura
Dues for the Repose, From Words Much Like Poetry

This book is dedicated to
Betty Jean Allen, my
mother who is the reason
that the beat still goes on.

And Tyaja Allen, my
daughter who made me
recalibrate my beat so that
I could go on.

TABLE OF CONTENTS

‡

ARISEN   7

CROWN ME   10

THE TELEVISION IS BROKEN   11

LET'S MAKE SOMETHING HAPPEN   14

OPEN WOUND   17

LIFE SUPPORT   19

WE STAYED   22

DNA MYTH   25

CAN'T BLAME IT ON MOTHER   27

EVERYBODY'S GANGSTA   30

TIT FOR TAT   32

SNIPERS   34

HIP HOP   36

PUT A GR ON THAT ATTITUDE   38

UNLOCKED PALATE   40

ECSTATIC   42

GENUINELY CONCERNED   44

WE HAD TO GIVE HER BACK   46

DOUGIE'S LAST STOP   48

ARISEN

my stunt double once told me
that if you learn how to fall
you'll always be able to rise again

Phoenician properties were internally placed
I contemplated that voice as another came
from the holy bible in my lap

and yet another from the crack pipe in my mouth.

they say the Phoenix rose from the ashes
I guess I used those same ashes
to clog the holes in my pipe

transforming chemical
changing rock to smoke
I didn't just fall to the bottom, I dissolved what I was

destroyed by the fire of a 50-cent lighter
that never held enough fluid
to complete my transformation.

paranoia continuously dropped me to my knees
to survey the crack under the door
saw so many shadows, feet moving

house was empty, besides me.

while on my knees, I prayed that no one
was around to stop me
from the cowardly suicide race, I was running

on the other hand, the bible was there for show
so, when someone did discover me
trying to disintegrate into ash to rise again

they'd see the tears of salvation
through the death of another.
there are too many beings present with no crowd control

the security guards have left the building
hold on, sacrifice one being to save another?
maybe I'm confused

you see I'm using the fire to burn the ashes
to melt my desire so that I may rise again
this is the cure all at work.

got a cold? take a hit.
got a fever? take a hit.
heart racing, chest jumpin'? take a hit.

couldn't comprehend the beginning from the end
the cloud from the combustion blinded me
kept falling and getting up
I was a Phoenix yo-yo

better than Duncan
this destructive toy touched mind, body, and soul
stunt double
            – the mind, crack pipe
            – the body, the bible
            – the soul

an aha! moment arrived
let us converse (must've been the bible talking)
the crack pipe said lay down, the stunt double said get up

the bible said do both but learn from your mistakes
my stunt double once told me that if you learn how to fall
you'll always be able to rise again

the yo-yo has stopped fluctuating
there's nothing afoot
the internal conversation has reached a standstill

so says "the Phoenix!"

CROWN ME

the things I see are rarely seen
because of the uniqueness of my vision
choosing to be a one of kind person is solely my decision
so now that the shell is broken, let's let the birdie out
spectators look on in anticipation,
a miracle on the horizon, no doubt

the conception of this new being
mixing the fruits from the loins of the gods
caused torrential rain, the sound of thunder,
peals of lightning shooting out in rods
a celestial occurrence, the orbs will move with grace
rearranging the hierarchy to prepare the rightful place

the constant changing of the guard,
the spiritual DJ plays the beats
a standing ovation is in order,
everyone rise up out of your seats
no grand entrance necessary, confidence rules the day
as I arrive to claim my throne, there's no comparison anyway

the aura is set on ultra-high, the coyness set on low
if I didn't mention I was bashful,
you wouldn't know, so take a gander at my gait,
marvel at the balance of the weight
you may not be cognizant of it at all
because this is an individual trait

so may the trumpets start to sound,
and the chimes continue to ring
I don't care who you think is entering,
but in my heart, I am king!

THE TELEVISION IS BROKEN

I'm cracking up right now!
because the system that is systematically
changing to shift the tide
of the one whom everyone deems a supreme being
is actually in the works
not that it will succeed
but the wheels have brought it to fruition
that bigotry has become the lesser of two evils
for control of an office whose prominence
is in the eyes of the people who created it
I vote that the vote doesn't even make a difference
the real rulers of this world have yet to surface
and I'm not talking about the Illuminati, yeah I said it!
so, let the killing continue!

because there are waves and waves of successors
that suppressors don't even know about
the plan has backfired
see the kings are hidden among the suppressed,
oppressed
so far buried that their rising will be surprising
even to themselves
the third eye opens and knowledge found becomes wisdom
who's going to stop it now?
so, let the killing continue!

because it hasn't worked yet
the rising and the uprising can be seen on the horizon
which means the order to eradicate is near
let's see what can be gotten rid of, whole genetic lines?
not when there are concubines
who produce geniuses on a regular

it's not the education that's sought
but the miseducation not thought
revealed through another outlet created to out society's secrets
social media and the "Enemy of the State Syndrome"
has opened sealed racist qualities of neighbors and friends
reveal yourself so when the king steps to the platform
we know where to take the fight
the underestimation has already been embedded

in years of slavery and acts to change the way it is portrayed
amendments to the constitution and the laws
that preach equality about how lower class
and upper class could be as one
picture that!
but the outlook is changing and it may take a lot of blood
which at least will be shed willingly
and not the "stop resisting" puppetry
of one's arms being jerked to feign movement
of the captures so that they may be caged or killed
so, let the killing continue!

the Phoenix is stirring in the ashes
left by constant actions that preach supremacy
of co-dependent beings
who without the lesser could not be great
can this actually go on without the oppressed?
who would be the next bothersome sorts?
the world leaders would turn on each other with greed
knowing in their upbringing that there is not enough to share
I may be looking out at the new king
or you may be looking back at him
all I know is that the race for dominance
will not be settled at the polling place
but the door will be open
for a live uprooting of society as we know it

some will sit back and watch
but somehow, I think
I will be a participant
whether I want to be or not!

LET'S MAKE SOMETHING HAPPEN

are you sitting there
    letting the doldrums of politics
        get you down

I'm here to tell you that gratefulness gets around
    let's start off slow thinking
        about the things we don't own

then pick up the pace
    thinking about how we have grown
        see if you don't give negative any energy,
            it cannot live

and the death of negativity
    is definitely positive
        it's sad that the heroes of the day
            are the ones who show monetary gains
            by selling poison

the real wars are fought in the trenches
    by those unseen
        a new type of veteran's day,
            we've escaped the guillotine

the sniper's bullets have mysteriously missed us
    but we still complain loudly
        and put up a fuss
            against spirits that promote idiocy

see we can only use band aids for the outside wounds
    we need spirituality to keep off the Devil's goons
        you must be aware to become ignorant

and you must acquire knowledge
to be heaven sent

we create these walls around us
and the sides are sinking in
already wondering how it's going to defeat us,
not thinking we could win

in other words, earn your keep,
before there is a whole block sweep
make sure you're taking a legal prescription
so the authorities can't say you fit the description
let me tell you, I'm not the store brought model
I have positive attributes that can be sold in a bottle

you are the president of your own united state
put the motion in action,
don't sit around and wait

you see I've become a mental assassin
with a verbal razor blade
thought process and language
is what I've displayed

be thankful for whatever happens
whether it pleases you or not
your character shows by your actions

when the kitchen gets hot
image goes out the window,
reputation makes no plan
it's now you all alone,
against the world
you must stand
let's make something happen

self-inventory is most important;
anybody can snap like a camera
but the picture that's developed
may look nothing like the negative!

keep thinking, keep monitoring, keep changing
and together,
let's make something happen!

OPEN WOUND

it's not something to be tampered with
proper care is definitely a must
not anyone can perform the work
it needs a mother's trust
stop piling on ingredients
in an attempt to heal it fast
because a rush for a scab to form
has a minimal chance to last

when taking the proper precautions
and using deterrents to ward off infection
the band-aid produced is spiritually applied
and is of maximum perfection
a molehill into a mountain
is a saying I've often heard
the smallest infraction can become a major wound
when proper affection is deterred

there is a wound residing here
but it's something you can't see
I hide it well and carefully change the dressing
so on the outside you still see me
although it's slowly closing
and the pain will slowly subside

I must continue to choose the proper 1st aid
want no more tickets to this ride
I can feel the scar as it forms
negative forces provide resistance
I've expanded my TLC team membership
to bolster my assistance

I hope I make the proper choices
and the scab a reminder in the end
my 1st aid kit consists of angelic souls
and hopefully will never open again!

LIFE SUPPORT

the focus should be on the present
even though the future lies in wait
the people who show the children love
can also teach them hate

our pedestals are only temporary
but children's hearts can be all in
the future is the parts
that we install when construction begins

to interact with beings
whose paths are not yet paved
with patience and a little understanding
their lives could be saved

or at least spared for a moment
with consequential thinking instilled
so when there's a choice between good and evil
they won't be instantly killed

knowledge is retaining information
wisdom is putting it into play
decision making is key in life
just to live another day

everyone take a look around this room,
these duties fall upon you
awards are given to the recognizable ones
but there are some unknown givers too

recognize just who you are
and step up to the plate

influence the youth around you positively
before it becomes too late

no negative newspaper articles
or commentary about the loss of life
let's teach them how to defend against it
not how to use the knife

let's not only teach them what they shouldn't do
let's teach them what they should
throw can't out the window, say yes, it's possible
and let them know they could

we're all intricate pieces of a puzzle
that have to work together to complete
the preparation of each little precious body
that comes across our seat

I don't know what happened to the village
but the components are still here
to improve a child's statistics
through every given year

let me say congratulations
to all who are honored here today
you've stood out in someone else's eyes
which shows that you paved the way

our children are the future
I hear this all too often
also hear how gifted they were
when lying in a coffin

I know this job is tiresome
and the pay ain't all too great

but the benefits are out of this world
when a child's success is fate

in closing, I would like you to keep in mind
to make every second count
towards what you add into each child's mind
because it is to what they amount

keep giving!

WE STAYED

what you see before you are
the ones who stayed home
took hold of responsibility
when it was so easy to roam

soaked up positive and negative
without any doubt
that they were destined to return
even if they were thrown out

let's talk about the bond
between father and child
in a world full of frowns,
it's the enticement to smile

there are no do overs in the parenting world
you have to cherish every moment with your boy or your girl
instill a code of ethics and morals, to boot
so they can verbalize in conflict and don't have to shoot

introduce them to spirituality in your own kind of way
so when the evil starts meddling they won't easily sway
give them everything without spoiling, easier said than done
teach them about friendship and who's the most important one

assist them with confidence so their ego is tamed
teach them about conmen so they're not easily gamed
when all is said and done and it seems your family team is
winning
let me notify you that this is only the beginning

no wonder some run

on the I'm pregnant announcement
but want to smoke cigars
on the it's a girl or boy pronouncement

that's the ones that want to look like good fathers
but they really are jerks
now listen up closely
if you want to put in some works

we aren't supposed to cry,
but we should be ready to die
and in some cases,
be ready to fly

because when your family is in need,
if they bleed, you bleed
your willingness to do this is important,
take heed

you're constantly called on,
and when laying down, crawled on
and when the mother don't like you
believe me you're stalled on

because you're the foundation of your own creation
our children are the builders of this new generation
you'll meet boyfriends and girlfriends, gay friends and bi
friends
some who may stay friends and claim ride or die friends

you'll deal with emotions and teenage love potions
disappointment, depression, anger, aggression
when does the fun begin
and this is before they reach ten

your selfishness is out the door
what you think you need,
the kids need more

you see i'm just brushing the surface
trying to spread knowledge
about this job we are doing,
not taught in any college

in the back of all father's heads is
I do whatever is necessary
never doubt our ability
because it's quite the contrary

I don't know about you
but I say don't mess with mine
I believe in this though,
we're one of a kind

we are also in unison
by taking the hand we were dealt
and coped with the fear
that we at one point felt

we looked at our hands
and with the cards properly played
we gave thanks to our higher power
and the people who prayed

which gave us the guidance
for the foundation we laid
fellas we're here because running was not an option
so we manned up and stayed!

DNA MYTH

participating in a child's life
        can be detrimental to their futures
see, we're trying to build leaders

and although women have taken a giant step forward
        the population of men is being eliminated
not only by black on black crime,
        misuse of force, and health issues
but by fatherly instincts never being instilled
        in our young men

the young ladies without fathers
        sometimes develop a hatred of men
which damages their future relationships
        and continues a cycle of families not being together

fellas, if the opportunity presents itself
        and you're not a willing participant
in your child's life
        as Maury would say, you are not the father!

99.9% DNA my ass
        as I look out among us
I see the cream of the crop
        the men on top, the game don't stop

it has only changed to compensate for a child
        in need of direction, who looks for affection
and that undaunted feeling of a father's connection
        "I love you Daddy," from a child's mouth
removes the myth that it can no longer be done
        that time one on one

it may seem like work to you
>   but in the end for them fun

stand up fathers and take your place
>   let's continue to prove to the human race

that we can keep pace
>   and that look on our face

shows the struggle of the professions we juggle
>   like when in turmoil we still have to snuggle

the goal is to be there even when elsewhere

let the thought remain that we're removing the stain
>   of a generation lost in pain

I see the letter "S" on chests
>   I see huge green monsters shape

when we think of our sons getting jumped
>   or our daughters getting raped

superheroes we are, we're not villains by far
>   and mistakes will be made

but foundations will be laid
>   so even when not present

our debts will be paid

I want to say thank you
>   for the strength some have shown

taking the responsibility to teach the unknown
>   so when they become grown

you won't be on your own
>   and celebrations rewarding fathers

will continue to be shown
>   that no matter what the DNA says

stand up because "you are the father"

CAN'T BLAME IT ON MOTHER

you see, mama ain't raise no fool
a few crazy people, yes, but no fool
there are individuals in this world today
that are the driving force of the human race
look around at the daily struggle of placing
the information where it is most valuable in our brains

your kids are crazy, not by any fault of yours
but because of the love you've shown
you see I'm gonna say we because I'm included
in the untreated. you better not give my kid no medication
ADHD, personality disorder, schizophrenic society
Ritalin in the form a leather strap or tree branch
we had to pick it out
they whooped your butt for talking back to the teacher
the I didn't curse type parents
but we can't blame it on Mother!

I remember hearing, "stay away
from those fast girls or those nasty boys"
having children at that age
when we weren't even finished partying yet
wacky weed, white powder, and alcohol
fueled our childhoods
some later than others
some parents would rather you did it at home
than get caught in the staircase with your friends
"I told you not to hang with that crowd"

there used to be beat cops
        (Smitty, Terry, Simmons, Clemens,
        and Robocop Haynes)

but the real patrollers were the "Mses."
     (the Pettiways, the Evans,
       and all elders on their respective blocks)
personally, I'd rather get caught by the cops

we knew ways to avoid
them but could never really hide
they always said, "wait until you have kids of your own"
we didn't listen
and we can't blame that on Mother!

some became slaves to incarceration
others to addiction
and some just couldn't find their way
out of the neighborhood
and if they did, they would always know
they could fall back on Mama
I just want to say look around
at the great job you did
we're damaged to a point
but we cope with problems now
that cause suicidal thoughts in others
we grew strong and learned from our mistakes

here we stand
the products of your hard work
yeah, we crazy
but we got your back
we've had our breakthroughs
though some have not yet learned their lessons
they will in due time
and there are others that may never learn
and we must continue to pray for them
lest they die in the streets

but just remember if they do
there is no way
you can balme it on Mother!

take the word blame and say it three times
then take the "M-E" off the end
and all you're left with is blah blah blah
so keep talking and not listening
keep blaming and not acting
all I know is that whatever befalls you
is because of...

Y our reactions to the stimuli in this world
O   say whatever you want, but on my word
U   can't blame it on mother!

EVERYBODY'S GANGSTA

>   your reputation
> exceeds
>   your character

the image of badness
not the true you
                    as a matter of fact
          the mistake in your image
has you scared of you
true blue

living off of someone else's rep
if you lose a fight
          they have your

>   **d**|b
>   **ʁ**|a
>   ɔ|c
>   **ʞ**|k

but for you to back
someone up you need a gun
          because of the fighting skills you lack

               see, you're not
          an up
front
          fighter
your weapon is your heart
when unarmed
          and not in a crowd
          15 deep
your gangsta seems to depart
showing aggression

when confronting women

but when it's a guy
~~speak~~

a real **man** deals with other men accordingly
when it comes to women, they are meek

careful what you listen to
rap music
is not your life
half that shit is made up anyway
you'll be in jail as someone's wife
your family
are the bad ones

but let's not be mistaken
in this world of guns and knives
anybody's life can be taken

so, heed this warning
gain some wisdom
give yourself a chance
to
grow
old
and remember not everybody's gangsta
they're just playing a role

TIT FOR TAT

an eye for an eye was a fair trade off at best
a gun duel settled things once and for all in the old west
or did it actually?

as the outcome lingered on the fringe
who was watching, concerned for the loser
already planning revenge
how far is it actually taken?
how vicious can it be?

it never stops with an individual person
take out the whole family

the mourning continues to get greater
as each new person dies
this cataclysmic repercussion
has the murder rate on the rise

        tragedy
    causes
feelings

hits like a tidal wave
be careful how you let your feelings
allow you to behave

retaliation turns to terrorism
the killing may never cease
forgiveness is easier said than done
why can't there just be peace
the person that does the initial killing
should be punished by the law

but I understand thinking that is not enough
and laymen must do more

just think that if this continues
everyone will get involved
because we're all somehow tied to one another
even though some of us have evolved
this could be a soap opera

the story goes

        on
            and
                on

it can even be taken up
in the future years
with every generation born
but think about the final outcome
the end of the thriller
where everybody in the world   besides you
                is dead
you stand
         a
           l
             o
               n
                 e

the final killer

SNIPERS

off the grid, I go locator dark
then I'm accused
of being somewhere I'm not

convicted of a crime
for taking something I never sought.

stream "Enemy of the State" on a device near you
then you'll know that you (un?)willingly participate
in a rigged game of hide and go seek

mechanical eyes make walls evaporate
no location is secret.

radio-frequency ID my credit card number
read me from a satellite in space
you're in a program

and the world can recognize
and use your face

cellular tendencies monitored
YOU'VE CROSSED THE LINE
saying what you feel more and more

G-men are now gunnin'
Metrocard ain't workin'

EZ pass is on the blink
                    blink
                        blink

you've become a rebel
this is not what you were taught to think

Truman Show, Stepford life reasoning
let the overblown tweets and memes keep you believing
what the fixated newscasters tell you

never using your own mind
how do you navigate the matrix?

which color pill did you choose?
do you think it has a bearing?
on whether you win or lose?

I say screw the normality
I'm an oddball with my own rules

won't be burdened with being alike
I am not a mule
I'm starting my own School of Acting

title role, ~~Oscar gold~~, scratch that
I really don't care who's watching

not even the "Eye in the Sky"
"Big Brother" snipers who thought
I'd lay down and seek and beg like a good dog

Hip Hop

friends and heads from the neighborhood
roadie for position
"STEP OUTSIDE THE ROPES PLEASE"
fame, your five minutes
being down, part of the setup
speaker, you, turntables, mixer
amp, you, fan,
crates, you, speaker
can't stay still, huh?

blending of songs from
genres unheard
cohesiveness tight
fluctuation of hands
by the real musician
hey DJ, wanna play that song
keep me dancin' all night
unregistered movements
controlled by
mechanisms powered by
the hanging of extension cords

five floors deep
con-ed cheap
lamp-post generator
of the schoolyard sway
let's dance
let's dance to the drummer's beat
do the hustle
electric boogie shocking
break dancers' layman for b-boys
twirl body, motion blurs vision

freeze, position lock

crowd roars
take a bow
showmanship on a concrete stage
the cultured playground of song and dance.

Put a GR on that Attitude

I hear there's a reason for the season
but the commercialization of a holiday
brings about people pleasing
the selfishness and wanting has caused a big shift
like Happy Birthday my savior, now where's my gift

they say a gift is a gift
but no orthopedic shoes
they say it's the thought that counts
but give me something I can use
no matter your present, I won't refuse
but be on the gift return line

on the eyewitness news
so be thankful and grateful for life itself
take all unwanted gifts and put them on the shelf
get back to the party and the holiday cheer
and pass that gift on to someone else next year

I remember wanting G.I. Joe with the kung fu grip
and receiving an irregular sweat-hood
that was already ripped
some irregular underwear that shifted to the side
and my Apollo 3 speed bike, I never did ride

your present holdings in life
you must appreciate
or all of your blessings
for them you must wait
believing in something and trusting
is an intricate part
of any new venture you're about too start

so, remember the reason for the day
and why we are here
and with blessings from above
hopefully see you next year
so we can once again share blessings
and the grace we receive to live
remember be grateful just to be here

no matter what you give
no matter what I receive
I'm grateful and surprised
because the first gift I open daily
are my very own eyes!

UNLOCKED PALATE

this is not a poem
to impress anyone
this is not for my enjoyment
and not just for fun

it's not because I'm happy
it's not because I'm blue
this is strictly to let you know
how I feel about you

it's hard to explain
how during such a short time
how you're the main guest
in the hotel room of my mind

the door was never shut
but the entrance was blocked
the windows were down
but the clasps were not locked

there was only one way
like to twist then to slide
to break down all barriers
and find yourself inside

but that's where you are
I'm hoping you'll stay
don't let simple clashes
chase you away

when I think of you
there's a sensation I feel

it's like anticipation
of your favorite meal

you crave it, you yearn it,
you just can't wait
for this most delicious morsel
to just touch your plate

the comparison's perfect
if you were the entree
I'd savor your flavor
for the whole damned day

one day this will happen
you'll come to my table
your mind will be cleansed
you'll be willing and able

to become one with me
until you say when
that's the only time
I'll call it the end

I'm hungry for your love!

ECSTATIC

my mind paints a picture
of you and me entwined
formed 69
I tongue tickle your fancy
you blow my mind

your nub betwixt my lips
baby fat as hand grips
undulating hips
your moan barely audible
my heartbeat skips

your mouth wide open, no speak
bed loudly creak
like on cocaine you tweak
as I anxiously guzzle
you leak

your attentive fixation
has no expiration
no need for oration
mouth skilled in writing
take perfect dicktation

together our portrait complete
liquid mixes when we meet
from our skulls to our feet
appetite suppressed
didn't we both just eat?

it just gets better
both wetter and wetter

did you swallow? I did
that's nutty, together?

we bask in the glow
of the remnants of flow
we produced during the show
our colors blended together
you already know

if I had my say
we'd stay this way all day
always ready to play
ecstasy between the sheets
as we lay, as we lay

GENUINELY CONCERNED

(A dedication to my late aunt, Ann Burroughs)

as we travel through life
general greetings are heard
how're you doing, how you feel,
what's up, what's the word

as I recall the personality
of who we celebrate today
let me tell you when she asked,
it was done in her own way

see the care that she showed
in her daily conversation
was really to assist you
with your tribulations

she would subtly correct you
if she thought you were wrong
but be caring of your feelings,
change the tune of your song

I remember as a child
the playground, her house
she'd give us this look
that would silence a mouse

feed you with input
and show you the big picture
and if all else fails
she'd hit you with scripture

I think of the discipline

that she wielded at home
I see the results in her children
now grown

the church, her second home,
where the lessons were taught
if you needed some counseling,
this is where you were brought

I took something from her
that nobody knew
I've used it and used it
until in my spirit it grew

when you ask of one's welfare
in god's memory it's burned
don't do it to just be nosy
but be generally concerned!

We Had to Give Her Back

(A dedication to my late other mother, Wilma Cameron)

as the tears continue to flow
we gain understanding so that we would know
because it's an understanding that we lack
that we had to give her back
our selfishness reigns supreme
god failed us it must seem
but in order for her to reach paradise
we had to abandon our dream
that she would live forever
and forever we'd be together

but in order for her life to continue
her worldly contacts she must sever
I don't know about you
but I was promised life beyond here
and I know my time approaches
with every passing year
we're gonna have our turn at this
so we must continue to prepare
if you knew anything about this woman
you'd know she was already there

if we had the last say in this
we'd probably say "Lord take us and let her live"
but then we would rob the rest of the world
of the gifts we have to give
see it is written that this is not our plan
and when God reaches down his hand
he picks up people and deems them kings and queens
and removes them from this land

our bodies are just the vessel
our souls are just on loan
our lives here on earth must move on
when our loved ones are called home
we all mourn in different ways
let's not talk about each other
let's form a bond look past our biases
support your sisters and brothers
this was exclusively put together
temporarily say goodbye
to this woman who touched more than a million hearts
and barely had to try

I bare true witness to this
and I'm sure everyone agrees
but her passing is not a captive moment
in fact, it actually frees
it releases her to have no worries
and live life without a care
think about the angels we have watching over us
she has a motley crew up there

I hope I've accomplished a few things while speaking
this was done with a purpose in mind
the first was to look out for each other
to your neighbor be kind
the most prominent was to give honor to Wilma Cameron
her served her Master well while in her earthly life
and it was just her time to go
the third was to point out that God's in control
and hopefully that's an understanding we no longer lack
so let Him use her in her heavenly life
and let us gracefully give her back!

Dougie's Last Stop

(A dedication to a late friend, Douglas W. Archer)

on first sight a transit worker seemingly on his way
with a blue bandanna proudly as a neck display
the first word out of his mouth was a thunderoous roar
and each sentence that followed, the volume became more

the rising crescendo could be deafening to the ear
you would think that as he aged
the decibels would decrease by year
believe it or not it didn't lessen, it actually increased
you can still hear his screams even though he's deceased

he argued his point because he knew he was right
and always left gracefully when his belly was tight
"that food was really good and the company was fun,
I'd just like to say I don't like to eat and then run"
but as he put on his coat and stood to his feet
he would always say "but I'd hate to run and don't eat!"

on this last leisurely stroll towards the heavenly gates
Dougie was still dougie not knowing his fate
MTA hat tipped to the booth clerk
as he moved towards the gate
he knew he was entitled and didn't have to wait
he dug in his pocket for his ride all year pass
and opened his wallet and proceeded to flash
when he was suddenly halted by a strong angelic voice
saying "you're coming with me
and you don't have a choice"

before he could open his mouth and declare he was free
and could do whatever he wants

and be whomever he wants to be
the voice shut him down and that's not easily done
he warned him to keep quiet stating "I'm not the one!"
"your train is about to leave
you follow and I'll lead
these earthly belongings you'll no longer need

"see Dougie you don't need your transit badge
to pass through the gate today
because the legacy you left
has already paved the way."

For information regarding featured readings and general author appearances, please visit our website.

www.urbancentigrade.com